INTRODUCTION

What happens when a relationship with a narcissist leaves you in a life-changing situation? When an event sends you into an uncontrollable spin? What happens when an incident blows your world apart, leaving you nowhere to hide and facing the desolation of a broken heart? The impact of a momentous event can leave the devastating realization that life will never be the same again. There's no immunity against grief; it's a very real pain that initiates the recipient into a courageous group of people who have endured pain and survived.

Life seems to start all over again from a point of no return, leaving a sense that there's only one direction to go – as far away as possible from the painful event, through the passage of time.

I spent many years trying to work out why grief can feel so powerful and overwhelming. Grief can be horrifying and disabling, and it should never be wished upon any soul. I have done my best to offer suggestions of short-cuts to end the trauma in this book.

I'm not a medical professional nor a counselor of any description. My only qualification is that I suffered at the hands of a narcissist and grieved heavily for many years. I had to find a way to move on from my pain and still manage the daily tasks of work and home. Being highly practical, I researched ways to work through trauma so I could get my life back to normal. My life and my mortgage depended on it.

This book outlined the strategies I used to help my own recovery based on many hours, days and years of researching, understanding and finding ways to move through the impacts of narcissist trauma. I have written it in the hope you can find a way to nurture yourself back to a newer, wiser and deeper you.

Peace, prayers and recovery,
Michelle Gregory

Guide to

Narcissistic Abuse Recovery

A science-based guide to heal
your relationship trauma

TABLE OF CONTENTS

CHAPTER 1

WHAT IS NARCISSISM?

Before I learned the word 'narcissism', I had experienced painful trauma with very few words to describe the offender. After a discussion with a colleague, I blurted out that I had encountered continual abuse from a monster. I devoured every personal story of anyone who cared to share their painful relationship experiences. One day, I heard the word 'narcissist'. I furthered my research into this new word and suddenly, the doors of knowledge flew open. I now had many words to explain why I had suffered so deeply. Narcissism is a psychological term that refers to a personality trait characterized by an extreme preoccupation with oneself. This mental health condition is named after the Greek mythological figure Narcissus who fell in love with his own reflection in a pool of water. It is defined in the American Psychiatric Association's Diagnostic and Statistical Manual of Mental Disorders, Fifth Edition (DSM-5) as a cluster B personality, Narcissistic Personality Disorder (NPD).

Individuals with narcissistic traits often have an inflated sense of their abilities and achievements, and they may constantly seek attention and praise from others to maintain their self-esteem. They might also have a sense of entitlement, expecting special treatment and privileges. Narcissists tend to lack empathy and have difficulty relating to other people's emotions and experiences. This emotional disconnect can be the catalyst for relationship strain, confusion and increased stress in partners.

Narcissism can range from mild to severe. While some levels of self-interest and self-confidence are healthy, excessive narcissism can negatively impact their relationships with others.

Common effects of narcissism include but are not limited to:

- **Relationship difficulties:** Narcissistic individuals often have difficulty forming and maintaining healthy relationships. Their excessive need for admiration, lack of empathy, and self-centered behavior can strain relationships and lead to conflict as they prioritize their own needs and desires over those of their partners. They may also exploit or manipulate people.

- **Lack of emotional intimacy:** Narcissists can struggle with intimacy as they often have difficulty connecting with others on a deep emotional level. This can result in shallow or superficial relationships, leaving them feeling unfulfilled and lonely.

- **Manipulation and exploitation:** Narcissists may use charm, flattery, or manipulation tactics to control or exploit others for their own gain, without considering the feelings or well-being of those around them.

- **Low self-esteem:** Paradoxically, narcissists often have fragile self-esteem and rely on external validation to feel good about themselves. They might constantly seek attention, praise, and admiration to boost their self-worth while deep down they feel insecure and inadequate.

- **Lack of empathy:** Narcissists typically have a limited capacity for empathy, making it difficult for them to understand or relate to their partners or loved ones' emotions and experiences. This can result in a lack of emotional support and understanding in relationships.

- **Impact on mental health:** Narcissism can also have negative effects on the mental health of individuals displaying narcissistic traits. They could have trouble managing their emotions, maintaining healthy self-esteem, and forming authentic connections. In some cases, narcissism can be associated with other mental health conditions, such as depression, anxiety, or personality disorders.

Red flags in a relationship are warning signs or behaviors that can indicate potential problems or issues. You might have noticed or sensed that there was something not quite right or unusual about the narcissist. Situations could feel strange or unsettling in ways you can't pinpoint or fully understand. Common red flags include:

- Lack of communication
- Controlling behavior
- Disrespectful or abusive behavior
- Lack of trust
- Unresolved conflicts
- Lack of support or empathy
- Manipulation

The impact of a narcissist's behavior can vary depending on the severity of narcissistic traits, from hurling insults that emotionally hurt to more brutal behaviors resulting in trauma-related illnesses in their victims.

Manipulation is one of the narcissist's greatest tools and is often referred to as *gaslighting.* The term originated from a play and subsequent film adaptation called *Gaslight,* in which a husband manipulates his wife into believing she is losing her mind by dimming the gaslights in their home and denying that any change has occurred. This is a form of psychological manipulation in which an individual intentionally tries to make someone doubt their own mental health.

In such a scenario, the narcissist may employ a variety of tactics to undermine the victim's confidence and sense of reality. Gaslighting typically involves tactics such as denying, guilt-tripping, blaming, distorting facts, projection and deflection, lying, trivializing, and contradicting the victim's experiences or emotions. The goal is undermine the victim and gain control over them. This assertion of control is a part of the deeper psychological complexity of the narcissist's mind. The feeling of power over another person feeds their self-entitled desires and fulfils their hidden agenda.

Gaslighting can have severe emotional and psychological effects on the victim, leading to self-doubt, anxiety, and confusion, along with a diminished sense of self-worth. Over time, the victim may become increasingly dependent on the manipulator and lose trust in their own perceptions.

Recognizing gaslighting behavior is crucial for protecting yourself and maintaining a healthy sense of self-worth. However, the covert behavior of a narcissist is not readily apparent and can be disguised in hidden meanings and underlying agendas. Outsiders won't notice their schemes, but you'll eventually start noticing a pattern and making connections as you piece together information and events. You'll uncover deeper meanings in their uncaring intent of manipulation and realize that their goal is to gain power by controlling their victims.

CHAPTER 2

THE PAIN OF BETRAYAL

A betrayal has taken place. You have been left feeling shattered by a continual barrage of abuse from a narcissist. The abuse hits you hard. You weren't expecting a relationship to feel this way.

When it ends, it hurts like mad. What should you do? What *can* you do? It feels like you need to explode, implode, or even lash out at the cause of your pain.

Regular expressions we hear every day become like monsters screaming their message:

Life will never be the same.
I'll never get over this.
What's happening to me?

Platitudes may come flowing in from people who care and people who *think* they care. Sometimes, these comments can help, but they do little to lessen the pain. These people don't understand the abuse you've endured.

At their best, platitudes give you some insight into the person who's delivered those meaningless words of comfort. They indicate genuine concern that you are hurting, but they're not sure how to offer deep, legitimate advice.

At worst, platitudes highlight the distance between you and the speaker's understanding of your predicament. Comments such as "you'll get over it", "it wasn't meant to be" or "toughen up" can add to your pain. But these comments are useful indicators of the people you need to avoid while you're still whirling from your pain.

Having a relationship with a narcissist is life-changing, and not what you'd dreamed about at the beginning of your romance. Over and over, the same question will circle your mind:

What do I do from here?

First, your priorities can feel like they have been changed beyond repair. You didn't choose to be in this place. The decision was made for you after you'd endured months or years of abusive behavior. You've suffered irretrievable losses financially and to your self-esteem, relationships with friends and family, and your reputation.

This is why you're angry. A change was made without your consent, leaving you vulnerable and devastated. You may be entering the *grief cycle*.

The grief cycle applies to anyone who's suffered a tragic loss. This can happen in anyone's life at any moment. It can be due to a death, crime, illness, or the end of a relationship. We usually learn about the grief cycle through our own individual experiences. Some people discover it early in life, others later.

First shock, then denial appears. Anger may follow. As these intense emotions grow, you may want to bargain with the universe to ease your pain, promising to never again be with someone as selfish as your narcissistic ex-partner. This could never happen again, could it? Surely, there could not be anyone else out there as callous and selfish as them who could do or say the things they did and said to you?

You promise the universe you will try harder never to be that vulnerable again. Depression may creep in as you realize what's been taken from you – money, time, and opportunities. After an arduous period of pain and isolation, hopefully, you'll feel a sense of change and will be able to move in a new direction, accepting your painful past and looking forward to a new future.

The grief cycle follows these stages:

- **Stability:** A state of innocence, calm before the storm.
- **Immobilization:** Shock and disbelief.
- **Denial:** Trying to shake off the event and 'this can't happen to me' beliefs.
- **Anger:** Realization of the loss and how this reality can't be changed.
- **Bargaining:** Pleading for mercy and a break from the pain. Seeking out a fix and making deals with the universe.
- **Depression:** Exhaustion from anger and working hard to make it better.
- **Testing:** A shaky time. Be careful, this is a crossroad and can lead you back through the grief cycle again or through to the next step of liberation.
- **Acceptance:** The promise of a new life – the place I advocate does exist. This may be hard to believe when you feel as if your body is turning inside out!

These emotional states create a physical effect, and your emotional and psychological pain can impact your physical health. Emotional pain is deeply connected to physical pain.

Recovery from narcissistic abuse is a priority. Your body can enter a state of shock. Each symptom from the grief cycle can produce a physical reaction within you. Between the states of immobilization and anger, you might experience some frightening physical reactions:

- dizziness
- headache
- nausea and/or vomiting
- memory loss
- chest pain
- stomach pain
- back pain
- crying
- sleeplessness
- nightmares and/or hallucinations
- exhaustion

When you feel five symptoms or more from the list, the pain will impact your physical health. The longer the pain resides in your body, the more likely your brain's messenger chemical, glutamate, will reduce in quantity, leaving you feeling fearful, vulnerable, and incapacitated.

In the words of trauma expert, Dr. Bruce Perry:

Trauma robs the organism.
A wound has been created and your health is now compromised.

CHAPTER 3

HEALING THE WOUND

Let's take a closer look at the initial wound you sustained. First, you went into shock. Something happened over which you had no control, leaving you hurt and vulnerable. Then your body started to react to your emotional state. Simply put, the sequence is:

EVENT – EMOTIONAL SHOCK – PHYSICAL RESPONSE

The moments that lead to a change in your life attack your levels of comfort and trust, and your values, ideals, hopes, and dreams of the future. Not only has this relationship left you with an emotional shock, but other factors also linked with the abuse, such as social and economic loss, may push you further into a vulnerable state and add weight to your despair.

No wonder the pain you feel is incredible. It's not all in your imagination. It's not just an emotional hiccup you need to get over. There are very painful emotional and physical issues taking place inside you. Be prepared to face discomfort during this challenging time. The journey is hard, but by facing some truths, you will place yourself in an advantageous position.

The pain is real. This is where you plan your campaign to heal.

First, what are your physical symptoms? Put them under scrutiny. You know your physical symptoms are the result of your reaction to narcissistic abuse. Begin your campaign of healing by facing your trauma.

Trauma will insert itself into the history of your life. This is **unchangeable**.

Your life is set to alter because of your trauma. However, this is **changeable**. Your campaign to recovery involves addressing what's taking place inside your body.

All parts of your brain may have been impacted by narcissistic abuse; your limbic, cortex, midbrain, and brain stem. *You can start your recovery immediately by using these simple, easy to access strategies.*

Dizziness

Stress can trigger dizziness. Pay attention if you suddenly suffer bouts of dizziness. Even if you know your dizziness is related to narcissistic abuse, a trip to the doctor can help eliminate other reasons for dizziness, such as a brain tumor, infection or high blood pressure. Your breathing may be erratic over days, weeks or even months as memories flow in and out of your head, recalling the nightmare you once lived. Sudden flashbacks may jump out at any time, resulting in a change of breathing. Be aware of your breathing at all times. Nurture your body by ensuring your oxygen levels are kept at a healthy level.

Remember, straining while breathing is unnatural and should be avoided. Even when strong, overwhelming emotions are hammering you, the power you will feel as you tame the movement beneath your chest will bring the sense of control you desire and deserve. Maybe you couldn't control the effects of narcissistic abuse, but you can control your lungs and diaphragm.

If you'd like to improve your breathing, yoga is a great discipline that teaches healthy breathing using the art called *pranayama* (*prana* means life force and *ayama* means control). You can work out a breathing rhythm that reclaims your sense of safety. You can take healing oxygen out of the air and turn it into your life force, right here, right now!

Headaches

Tightness in your jaw, neck, back and shoulder muscles could cause you thumping headaches.

If this applies to you, circle your shoulders, then roll your head around gently and slowly. Hang your head forward, then back as if you're looking at the sky. Keep your eyes closed if dizziness has been an issue. Remember, stretches ought to be done for about fifteen seconds at a time to increase your flexibility.

Focus on what happens with each movement of your head and shoulders. Does your neck crack? Is there a pull in your shoulder? Has the emotional impact of narcissistic abuse shown up as a physical weakness, such as crooked hips, a drooped shoulder, or a rolled ankle? Any imbalance in your posture alters how your muscles fit with your skeleton, from your head down to your toes.

An emotional shock can cause tension, highlighting a need for a postural check. Good posture is vital for excellent health. Research shows that during postural adjustment, your brain will experience a shift in brain activity. Chiropractic care is an option you can investigate to resolve muscle tension.

Nausea and stomach pain

When under stress, your adrenal steroids (stress hormones) increase. Cortisol is one of these hormones and can compromise your stomach's health. Cortisol thinks it's doing you a favor by pumping energy to your vital organs so you can fight your battle. Your stomach is not a vital organ during battle, so it misses its usual dose of energy! Less energy means a lower digestive ability. Your stomach is left with the difficult job of doing an important task with very few resources. Go easy on your stomach. It's suffering too.

Try some easy-to-digest foods, such as oatmeal, beans, white rice, noodles, boiled chicken, bananas, ginger, or probiotic yoghurt drinks. Mashed potato and pasta are great comfort foods, as their complex carbohydrate power steps in to provide you with a boost of energy to get you through the day or night.

Memory loss

During a crisis, stress hormones can have a direct influence on your brain's health, especially your hippocampus, which controls your memories and emotional processing. Some studies show that the hippocampus can shrink from ongoing stress and depression! It's vital to confront the truth of what could be happening inside your brain.

Protect your brain by ingesting some fish oil as soon as you can. It's cheap and readily available in supermarkets and drugstores. Omega-3 fatty acids, associated with fish oil, concentrate in the brain and have been linked to cognitive functions, such as memory and behavior. In other words, omega-3 will protect your brain. If you have the budget, invest in fish oil that's refrigerated and kept in health shops. The higher quality of this oil brings huge benefits.

Most importantly, gain further information on fish oil from a health care provider if you have diabetes, have had an organ transplant, or are being treated for high cholesterol or a skin disorder.

Chest and back pain

When we're stressed, our muscles can become tense. Stress can cause an over production of adrenaline that hangs in muscles, causing them to tense to prepare for a survival surge. Having tense muscles is a warning sign that your stress hormones are taking charge and compromising your health. Watch for this before the tension becomes unmanageable. Although adrenaline burns off quickly, it may be an antecedent to the next imminent attack from other adrenal steroids.

Chapter 5 provides you with information on how to weaken the punch of these stress hormones. Surprisingly, this defense comes mainly in the form of food.

Crying

Crying about upsetting experiences releases corticotropin into your tears, which then exits through your tear ducts. Corticotropin is responsible for the secretion of cortisol, a stress hormone. Less corticotropin in your body means less cortisol. Part of your healing strategy is to reduce the amount of cortisol in your body.

Cry out corticotropin to lessen the amount of cortisol surging through your veins. Crying might feel uncomfortable, uncontrollable, and confining, but do it anyway, although you might want to place a time limit on your crying. If your crying is uncontrollable, you need to quickly move to the next strategy – support from a health professional.

Nightmares

In the dark of the night, when sleep comes, nightmares can arrive, infiltrating your dreams and replaying the narcissist's behavior. You could feel as if there's nowhere to hide. Even in your dreams, you are reminded of your brokenness.

Protect your sleep by employing sleep aids.

- Magnesium, found in legumes, seeds and leafy green vegetables, as well as supplements, is a muscle relaxant.

- Relax before going to bed, rather than partaking in over-stimulating activities, such as watching television.

- Hot baths will aid your sleep. Your body needs to cool down to sleep. Your body's internal thermostat system will work to pull down the heat in your body from the hot bath and this will induce sleepiness. The ideal bath temperature is approximately 102 degrees Fahrenheit (39 degrees Celsius), and you should take your bath no less than one hour before bedtime.

- Get some tryptophan into your body. Tryptophan is an essential amino acid that's associated with serotonin (a feel-good hormone) production in your body. Tryptophan is found in milk, peanuts, sunflower seeds and – you may be pleased to know – chocolate. I have listed tryptophan-rich foods in Chapter 4.

Hallucinations

Not everyone will experience these. However, if your narcissistic abuse has been extremely traumatic, hallucinations may appear. If this happens, call a health professional *immediately*!

Exhaustion

Overwork causes exhaustion, and your body has been overworking since the abuse took place. Your normal responsibilities don't stop while you're dealing with trauma, and you still have responsibilities. Trauma is an extra burden.

Stop, rest, and listen to relaxing music. Music can alter your physical state. A song by Symbiosis "Touching the Clouds" was found to be the most relaxing music played in a 1994 study at Kingston University. Other composers, including Kevin Kendle, Llewellyn and Tony O'Connor, have a natural talent for developing soothing music.

There's a school of thought that believes depression and anxiety reside in the right brain. By activating your left brain by completing logical activities, such as a sudoku or jigsaw, you can distract yourself from the overthinking, anxious side of your creative and sensitive right brain.

***

Now you have a definite set of physical symptoms to describe how you feel, you can develop a practical approach to a healing strategy. It's easier to treat stomach pain, sleeplessness or headache than a devastating emotion like anger, rage, or overwhelming sadness.

Let's recap the simple strategies you can use immediately to deal with grief:

- Breathe with focus
- cry
- Gently stretch any tight neck muscles
- Eat chicken with pasta or mashed potatoes, scoff down a banana, and heat up some baked beans when you need comfort food
- Start taking three grams of fish oil a day (or the recommended daily intake on the label)
- Get magnesium into your body
- Get tryptophan into your body
- Have a hot bath an hour before bedtime
- Stop, rest, and listen to relaxing music
- Have a spinal adjustment from a chiropractor (an x-ray may be required first)
- Distract yourself with left brain activities

You can now implement a series of strategies to address your trauma. This is only a start. These strategies are not going to bring an immediate escape from pain, and it takes more than eating a banana to triumph over your trauma. However, you're on the path to success once you've started your strategy of working through your trauma by searching for answers.

In this chapter, we have seen how shock from narcissistic abuse creates psychological and physical pain. We've explored possible physical symptoms of emotional shock and how we can begin to treat them with practical solutions. We can turn those critical moments of trauma into proactive strategies to minimize the impact of narcissistic abuse.

CHAPTER 4

TRAUMA AND THE
NERVOUS SYSTEM

E motional trauma from narcissistic abuse can undermine and immobilize the victim. A fun night out is a difficult activity for a wounded person to contemplate. Wounded people retreat to a place where they're safe; it's a natural response. We need a safe place to heal.

Your limbic brain senses your suffering and falls into panic mode, sending your body into the well-documented flight/fight challenge. Your limbic brain does not like discomfort. Its functions now are dedicated to turning your *discomfort* into *comfort*.

Translated into physical terms, your brain's limbic outburst has impacted on your hypothalamus, which controls your *central nervous system*, also called your *autonomic nervous system*.

Your central nervous system has two parts: your *sympathetic nervous system* and your *parasympathetic nervous system*. Your sympathetic nervous system can be described as *reactive* while your parasympathetic nervous system can be described as *soothing*.

Both systems have direct nerve connections into your organs and can create a reactive or soothing response in them. They run at a complementary pace to support your body in responding appropriately to your environment and will tell you when it's a suitable time to eat as you feel safe or a time to run when danger is near.

Narcissistic abuse activates your limbic brain and commands your hypothalamus to send instructions to your sympathetic nervous system to fight your discomfort and return it to the comfort you were once familiar with. Your sympathetic nervous system is a *physical nerve system* in your body. It responds to the changing point in your life using the evolutionary survival mode of flight/fight.

Your blood pressure, heart, and breathing rates increase; your vision and hearing become refined, and your stomach and intestines become less active. Other essential functions are suspended due to energy reduction, such as your immune system and the production of growth hormones. Therefore, your sympathetic nervous system is sympathizing with your case through physical responses.

As if narcissistic abuse is not humiliating enough, your hypothalamus sends a stress-releasing hormone to your pituitary gland that passes on the message in the form of the adrenocorticotropic hormone. This hormone activates your adrenal glands into producing the stress hormones adrenaline and cortisol. Narcissistic abuse stirs up the following process within you:

> Your distressed limbic brain activates your hypothalamus gland. Your hypothalamus gland activates your sympathetic nervous system's physical responses and your adrenal glands with stress hormones.

It's easier to focus your aim at your brain and central nervous system and apply techniques to reduce the impact of the fight/flight and stress hormone response than it is to search through the maze of confusion brought on by emotions such as sadness, anger, distress, bewilderment, rage, despair, misery, desperation, gloom and dejection.

CHAPTER 5

FEEDING YOUR BODY AGAINST TRAUMA

There's nothing classy about trauma. It is not an emotion that a night on the town can fix. It's a threat to your health. Narcissistic abuse can leave an indelible mark on your life.

The effects of trauma can take a turn for the worst when the reality of what you have endured sinks in. Disbelief about how you could be treated so badly can burn like a thousand demons running through your aching body, feeding off your pain and vulnerability. You need to snare these demons, tame them, and subjugate them before they swallow you up and leave you as a devoured carcass. The demons are real. They're not a figment of your imagination. The demons are *adrenal steroids* or *stress hormones*.

Adrenal steroids are necessary for blood pressure and sugar maintenance and your immune system's functioning. However, high doses of adrenal steroids over an extended period are harmful. When your adrenal steroids are left to run uncontrolled in stressful times, they can cause:

- Brain damage
- insomnia
- Weight gain and weight gain related diseases
- Calcium depletion
- A compromised immune system

Who'd have thought that narcissistic abuse could lead to an endangered immune system, as well as brain damage?

Too much activity from the hypothalamic-pituitary-adrenal axis results in an overload of cortisol (the main adrenal steroid), which can wear your body out. Rather than crying into your pillow with grief, now is a suitable time to think about how to protect your body from over-activated adrenal steroids.

Go easy on yourself – don't panic! Your body has been designed perfectly from going through a refinement process in your ancestors for hundreds of thousands of years, right up until the day you were born as a little bundle of evolutionary perfection.

You can take the power away from over-active adrenal steroids (especially cortisol) and tame them.

- Protect your brain with omega 3, which can be found in fish oil, broccoli, cauliflower, seeds, canola oil, milk, and eggs.

- Cut back your coffee – okay, don't quit caffeine if you love it dearly, but reducing your intake by one cup per day will make a difference to your cortisol (stress hormone) levels.

- Watch those sugary treats. Let's be sensible here; this is not a weight watching exercise, it's a treatment for grief. Adrenal steroids will de-stabilize the sugar/insulin relationship in your blood stream. You're battling a hormone that can cause weight-related diseases, so replace that donut with some tryptophan enriched foods.

- Research by Dr. Linus Pauling, 1954 Nobel Prize Winner, discovered the powerful effects of vitamin C. This super vitamin can lower cortisol levels! Vitamin C is found in kiwifruit, feijoa, guava, Kakadu plum, persimmons, and strawberries, and vitamin C powder can be bought in health shops. (If you choose to have your vitamin C intake through orange juice, drink through a straw to lessen the risk of cavities).

- Eat a phosphatidylserine supplement. Phosphatidylserine can aid in the decrease of the main stress hormone, cortisol, by as much as 39 percent! It has an amazing healing effect on our humble human brain. Phosphatidylserine has been scientifically proven to bolster cognitive improvement and other higher brain functions. This is hugely significant when you're battling stress demons. Originally, phospholipid supplements were made from cow brains but are now made from soybeans. You can also obtain phosphatidylserine from offal, lamb's kidney, chicken heart and liver, and Atlantic herring. Place phosphatidylserine supplements on your list of "must-haves."

- Invest in a bottle of ubiquinol (also known as CoQ10, or Kaneka). Research from Waseda and Tsukuba Universities in Japan found that taking 100 mg of Ubiquinol daily improved depression in the elderly.

- Investigate how the periwinkle flower can metabolize in your brain in semi-synthetic produced vinpocetine, a strong anti-inflammatory that enhances blood-flow to the brain. It activates cerebral metabolism and can enhance your memory and concentration.

- Have you ever heard of a flotation tank? Imagine lying in ten inches (25 centimeters) of salty water. It is dark and quiet. The water gently envelopes you at a pleasant 97 degrees Fahrenheit (36 degrees centigrade). This sensory experience is enough to induce your brain into a relaxed state. Floatation tanks were originally designed by Dr. John C. Lilly in 1954, who wanted to know how the brain would react under deprived sensory conditions. He discovered the opposite to his expectation that the brain would react as a deprived organ. The brain thrived under the peaceful, salty, and dark conditions of a floatation tank! Twenty-nine years later, researchers made a remarkable discovery involving floatation tanks. Professor T.H. Fine and Dr. R.A. Borrie found that hormones directly associated with stress (cortisol and epinephrine/adrenaline) decreased during restricted environmental stimulation therapy sessions. Search for the closest floatation tank in your town or city or recreate the sensation of a floatation tank by visiting your local swimming pool, closing your eyes, and floating your stress away.

- Food sensitivities and allergies have been linked to an increase in cortisol. Have a food allergy test to ascertain if any signs of stress can be alleviated.

Decrease the harsh effects of adrenal steroid, cortisol by:

- Eating omega-3 daily – fish oil capsules are effective and practical
- Cutting back your coffee by one cup per day
- Eating a phosphatidylserine supplement
- Ingesting vitamin C
- Avoiding sugar while your blood levels are potentially compromised
- Trying some sessions in a floatation tank
- Investing in a bottle of ubiquinol
- Investigate periwinkle flower's vinpocetine
- Having a food allergy test

Now you're using your inner evolutionary design to win back your life. Remember to:

- Cry
- Stretch gently any tight neck muscles
- Eat chicken with pasta or mashed potatoes, or eat a banana or baked beans
- Get magnesium into your body
- Get tryptophan into your body
- Have a hot bath an hour before bedtime
- Stop, rest and listen to relaxing music
- Eat omega-3 daily
- Cut back your coffee by one cup per day
- Take a Phosphatidylserine supplement
- Eat vitamin C
- Avoid sugar while your blood levels are potentially compromised
- Invest in a bottle of ubiquinol
- Investigate periwinkle flower's vinpocetine
- Try a floatation tank session
- Have a food sensitivity test

CHAPTER 6

FEEL-GOOD RESCUERS

Internally, we have our own internal rescuers. These rescuers are serotonin, oxytocin, and endorphins.

Serotonin is a neurotransmitter that's found in your intestines and your central nervous system. It promotes calm, sleep, and relaxation, and activates your parasympathetic nervous system.

Earlier, I mentioned how your response to the impact of narcissistic abuse activated your *reactive* sympathetic nervous system, which left you feeling stressed. Serotonin can kick start the other side of your central nervous system (your parasympathetic nervous system), which is the *soothing* aspect of your central nervous system.

Your brain uses the raphe nuclei (a cluster of nerve endings found in your brain stem) to pull out serotonin from your central nervous system. The raphe nuclei directs serotonin around the parts of your brain associated with mood, cognition, memory, and sleep. Serotonin plays a key role in creating happiness as it journeys from your intestines, through your central nervous system, then into your brain.

You can boost the production of serotonin in your intestines by ingesting tryptophan. (Your body can't produce tryptophan.) Tryptophan can be derived from certain foods, such as milk; peanuts; sunflower seeds; cottage cheese; dates; papaya; red meat; fish; poultry, chicken (especially chicken breast); egg white; oats; pineapple; asparagus; pork; tofu; parsley; mozzarella cheese; bananas; mung beans; lobster; mushrooms; and nuts.

It's a paradox that the impact of narcissistic abuse can feel like a kick in the stomach, and yet the starting point for healing is using the natural hormone found in our intestines – the very place we feel we have been kicked! Hippocrates (c.460-377 B.C.E.), the Greek father of medicine, told us "All disease begins in the gut" and "Let food be your medicine and medicine your food." Nobel Prize winner Elie Metchnikoff, a Russian biologist, made a more somber comment when he said, "Death starts in the colon [intestines]." Add life to your gut/colon/intestines by eating tryptophan-rich foods!

Endorphins are produced in the hypothalamus and pituitary gland, both found in our brain. Endorphins are opioid peptides and have a pain-killing effect on the body. The word *endorphin* is short for *endogenous morphine*, which alludes to the "high" produced by endorphins.

How do you produce your own endorphins? Breathe in, hold, and breathe out. Breathe in, hold, and breathe out. It's that easy. Your body may feel like it's gasping for air or not even breathing at all. But your breathing won't stop. You're designed to breathe, but you have the choice and the power to control the muscles that drive your lungs to open. Yoga teaches us that breathing should be calm and smooth. Keep your spine straight and breathe through your nose. To balance your nervous system, block one nostril as you breathe through the other. Then swap this process by blocking the opposite nostril and repeating the single nostril breath. You have been breathing all your life, so you're already an expert. Just for now, breathe a little deeper. Breathing really is that simple.

Chili peppers have the active ingredient capsaicin, which triggers the release of endorphins. Raise your endorphins to heavenly heights by eating chili foods!

Trial results published in *Journal of the American Medical Association* (September 2008) linked regular exercise in an improvement in memory function. Fit in a twenty-minute walk as a healthy benefit for a stressed brain.

Researchers from the University of Oxford found a group of rowers training together had an increase of endorphins. So, if possible, train with other people. Throw yourself around a soccer field, join a boxercise class, or play indoor cricket or netball and you'll find your endorphins will start pumping from your brain's wonder gland, the hypothalamus.

If group work is so praiseworthy for emotional/physical health, why not join an emergency rescue group? Train to abseil and wade through raging rivers while carrying stretchers. That will give your hypothalamus a reason to pump those endorphins! If physical activity is not your forte, you could work behind the scenes in communications for rescue squads. Imagine being at the center of a high alert situation where people's livelihoods are reliant on the work you do.

Amazingly, acts of kindness and xenial behavior can raise your endorphins. Researcher Alan Luk discovered twenty years ago that doing virtuous deeds creates a positive biochemical change in people, reducing their stress levels as well as producing endorphins. Leap into xenial behavior. Ask a friend over and shower them with hospitality. You will not only raise your endorphins but you'll also raise theirs as well. *By interacting with others, you can turn your I'llness into We'llness.*

Singing, laughter, a little bit of dark chocolate, acupuncture, meditation, and massage can all release endorphins. Of these six activities, which one can you arrange to take place within the next twenty-four hours?

Show kindness by giving something to someone. You can give to your community by donating blood to your hospital, donating items not needed in your house to charity, or by giving your time as a volunteer for a non-profit organization.

Produce your own supply of endorphins:

- Breathe for endorphins
- Eat chili foods
- Take a twenty-minute walk
- Work up a sweat in group exercise sessions
- Display xenial behavior, be kind, show hospitality
- Sing
- Laugh

- Eat a little dark chocolate
- Acupuncture
- Meditation
- Massage

Oxytocin is created from love and creates love! Whether you need to avoid love due to the trauma it's caused or saturate yourself in it to heal, oxytocin will work for you. It's secreted by your pituitary gland, which sits near the base of your brain. Oxytocin can aid intimate bonding between people, and create a growth of maternal feelings, trust, and empathy, and reduce fear. You'll feel more inclined to share your feelings with friends. Oxytocin promotes resistance to stress and, most importantly, increased levels of oxytocin correlate to lowered levels of cortisol.

Dr. Berit S. Cronfalk from the Stockholm Sjukhen Foundation, stated how gentle massage released oxytocin and gave relief to grieving families of relatives lost to cancer. Massage and the act of loving promote the production of oxytocin.

Oxytocin can come in a nasal spray. It may only be useful in the short term, but it would be wise to first discuss its use with a healthcare professional.

Your feelings of loss, betrayal, and trauma may still be entwined with feelings of love. Those feelings of love may feel too much of a reminder of your loss. But keep loving – keep producing oxytocin. Love is a verb, an action, and a deed. Love that friend, love that child, love that animal, love that favorite café where you can sit and people watch all day. Keep loving at all costs!

Strategies to implement immediately

Biochemical	Why?	How?
Increase soothing serotonin	Serotonin is a feel-good hormone and affects mood, memory, cognition and sleep.	Eat tryptophan foods: milk; peanuts; sunflower seeds; cottage cheese; dates; papaya; red meat; fish; chicken (especially chicken breast); egg whites; oats; pineapple; asparagus; pork; tofu; parsley; mozzarella; bananas; mung beans; lobster; mushrooms; and nuts.
Increase soothing endorphins	Endorphins are an endogenous morphine – a strong, natural painkiller.	Breathe deeply; eat chocolate; eat chili foods; take a twenty-minute walk; work up a sweat in group exercise sessions; sing; laugh; display xenial behavior with acts of kindness; have an acupuncture session; meditate; or have a massage.
Increase soothing oxytocin	Oxytocin reduces fear and aids in sharing feelings. It helps you build trust in relationships.	Love and keep loving, whether it is a pet, a child, a close relative or a friend. Have a massage.

Decrease reactive cortisol	Long-term exposure leads to brain damage, insomnia, weight gain and related cardiovascular issues, calcium depletion, and a compromised immune system.	Cry a little to release corticotrophin from your body; reduce your coffee diet by one cup a day; protect your brain with omega-3 (found in fish oil); consider taking phosphatidylserine, vitamin C, ubiquinol and vinpocetine supplements; experience a flotation tank; and have a food sensitivity test.

Religious worship can assist in healing from grief. Research supports the idea that having faith in a higher power can improve mental health and combat the disabling symptoms of depression. In democratic countries, people have the choice to pursue individual happiness through worship. There are many religions available to investigate to overcome emotional/physical pain:

- Hinduism
- Islam
- Judaism
- Christianity
- Buddhism
- Shinto
- Candomblé
- Bahai
- Taoism

There are several ways in which involvement in religion helps in dealing with trauma:

- Increased social contact
- Inspires feelings of hope
- Meditation and prayer offer a calming effect
- It creates a sense of belonging
- The work of powerful faith gives strength to the believer

CHAPTER 7

THE SOUND OF HEALING

T he roar of thunder announces the power of a storm. As warm air particles around lightning smack together, a brontide of power and vibration rumbles across the sky. The sound of thunder can vibrate at a low tone sounding like a heaven-sent lullaby, gently reminding us that the storm is passing onward to a distant land. There are times when thunder will vibrate with a seismic bellow, great enough to send us diving for cover. Thunder creates awe with its spectacular display of nature's most powerful, commanding exhibition.

Vibrations (like those produced in thunder), when harnessed and used at the correct oscillation, can serve a healing purpose in brain care. Here are a few examples that show vibrations can be used to heal:

- The works of Dorothy Retallack in the 1970s showed how plants grew toward soothing music and away from heavy metal music.

- Voodoo music was played to mice in 1998 by physicists Dr. Harvey Bird and Dr. Gervasia Schreckenberg. This group of mice had difficulty finding food in a maze compared to the control group. The neurons in their brain showed an unnatural branching-out pattern.

- Cats purring at a frequency between 25 and 150 hertz can keep their bones dense through the bio-mechanical action of their laryngeal and diaphragmatic muscles.

- The mystical sound of *Om* is the primordial vibration from which comes everything. Chanting Om is believed to lower blood pressure, slow down brain waves, and reduce cholesterol. Studies at Georgetown University found that regular chanting helped lower blood pressure after three months.

- A newborn baby cries while being rocked in your arms. What's one of the first things you do to soothe her? You gently whisper, "Shhh." What sound does the ocean produce as waves tumble landward? What's the sound of heavy rainfall? Both have a "shhh" quality to them? I use the sound "shh" in a gentle, soothing way in my classroom when students become loud and erratic. I have found it remarkable for calming and refocusing them. The sound, "shhh" has acoustic qualities very much like white noise – the sum of all sound frequencies oscillating together. White noise machines are sound for therapeutic purposes and can be a useful aid for a good night's sleep.

- Gregorian chants vibrating through the solfège scale are believed by many to possess healing tones. The solfège scale is UT (396 Hz), RE (417 Hz), MI (528 Hz), FA (639 Hz), SOL (741 Hz), LA (852 Hz). You may recognize this scale as do, re, mi, fa, sol, la, ti, do. The scale was first recognized in a Latin hymn written by Paulus Diaconus in the eighth century.

- A remedy to calm a new puppy that has left its mother is to wrap a clock up in a towel. The sound of the ticking clock replicates its mother's heartbeat, leading to a less anxious baby canine.

- A clock ticks at sixty beats per minute. Baroque music at sixty beats per minute was used by psychologist Dr. George Lazonov to encourage super learning with foreign language students. Dr. Lazonov's students experienced a huge rate of success from using his methods.

- Many health advocates believe the vibration from tapping the thymus gland enhances our health and well-being. Your thymus gland is in your chest behind your sternum, about three inches below your throat. It's responsible for taking t-cells made in bone marrow and incubating them to maturity before they're released as part of your immune system. Tapping can be achieved by using four fingers for thirty to sixty seconds. This area is known as K27 in acupuncture. Acupuncture releases *qi* which regulates spiritual, emotional, mental and physical balance according to traditional Chinese practice.

- Drums can be healing. Neurologist and author Dr. Barry Bittman discovered that group drumming sessions stimulated the production of cancer destroying white blood cells. Drumming has been used over thousands of years in many cultures for prayer, celebration, warfare, and healing.

Using the power of vibration, you can take steps to control the devastating effects of narcissistic abuse:

- Play soothing music
- Avoid heavy metal while healing
- Listen to or chant Om
- Listen to Gregorian chants
- Listen to baroque music, which has sixty beats per minute
- Tap your thymus gland
- Play your own drum, beatbox drum, or steel tongue drum
- Download apps for soothing music

CHAPTER 8

AMPLIFY YOUR BRAIN

With lightning comes growth in nature's powerful surge. With a rate of 1.4 billion strikes on Earth each year, lightning is responsible for producing the protective layer of ozone that shields us from the sun's deadly UV rays. Lightning breaks up environmental nitrogen, an essential component of DNA building blocks in our ecosystem. At the speed of lightning, invisible bio-chemical reactions take place, enabling all living things to survive on our planet.

Like lightning, our brain has electrical impulses. Invisible reactions take place at lightning speed, building and growing new synaptic connections. Once thought of as irreparable, the brain is now considered flexible. It performs *neurogenesis*.

Grow your own brain neurons by just thinking!

A prominent Berkeley professor, Mark R. Rosenzweig, taught students that thinking increased the number of dendritic branches in the brain. He also discovered that the brains of rats became heavier and thicker after enrichment activities.

Train your brainwaves into the ideal state!

Brainwaves, or electrical patterns, are measured in hertz from 0.1 Hz to > 40. These electrical patterns can become *entrained* with binaural beats. That means two auditory beats with a frequency derived from a mathematical formula from the outside environment enter the ear canal, travel down the auditory nerves which have a short pathway to the brain, then change the electrical pattern of the brain!

The alpha state is found at 8–13 Hz per second, the beta state at 14–60Hz per second, the delta state at 1–4 Hz per second, and the theta state at 4–7 Hz per second.

The theta state is associated with sleeping and dreaming. The ideal electrical state to experience a sense of calm from a rise in serotonin is in the alpha state at 8–13 Hz per second.

Is it a coincidence that Earth's natural electromagnetic waves beat at 7.8 hertz? It's startling to discover that 7.8 hertz marks the border between the theta and alpha states, which are optimum states for dreaming and deep meditation.

Yadav and colleagues assessed the use of brain entrainment technology to help teenagers cope with mental health issues. The intervention included thirty-minute meditation sessions and fifteen-minute brainwave entrainment sessions with binaural beats and isochronic sound therapy tones three times a week for four weeks. The findings of this study demonstrated positive outcomes for an increase in well-being.

Influence another person's brain? But wait!
They could influence yours!

Research by Trisha Stratford, neuropsychotherapist at the University of Technology, Sydney, discovered that two people can entrain their brain waves together so that they're both aligned with physiological coherence. This is when you may feel you're "at one" with another person. The part of the brain activated during this time is the parietal lobe, the part that sits at the top. People involved in this research have been shown to have lower levels of anxiety and lower heart rates.

In a sense, people can interact on a physiological level just by being near each other. Keep in the company of people who are calm, caring and relaxed, and enjoy synchronizing with their brain!

The new buzz word in neurology in recent times has been *neuroplasticity*. The brain can repair itself. By relearning, the brain can 'rewire' and heal itself.

Amplify your healing when you:

- Keep busy with enrichment tasks; activities that keep you thinking
- Listen to binaural beats and slip into soothing alpha brain waves
- Surround yourself with calm people and synchronize with their brain

CHAPTER 9

SELF-INVENTORY

When a light shines in dark corners, we see everything. Who are we? Do you know yourself? Have you shone a light on who you are? You have learned the processes of what can happen in your body and mind when caught up in narcissistic related trauma. By applying healing strategies to your body and mind, you can retain your true self. Now is the time to take an inventory of your character. Place yourself under the spotlight and illuminate the true part of yourself, your soul, using these reflective strategies:

Inventory 1: Create a personal year list

By focusing on one major event each year of your life in Inventory 1 below, you'll see how important each year of your life has been. I have started with an example.

Age	Event
0-12 months	For example, using this fictional identity: I was born in Marketville Hospital for Women at 3.55am to Lorraine and Jack Andrews, on the 23rd of September 1978.
1 year old	I took my first steps to Uncle Brent, much to my mom's dismay.
2 years old	Attended kindergarten
3 years old	Rode on a pony at Springfield Park annual fair
4 years old	Fell off my bike and scarred my knee.

Now, it's your turn.

Age	Event
0-12 months	
1 year old	
2 years old	
3 years old	
4 years old	
5 years old	
6 years old	
7 years old	

Inventory 2: Write a personal values list

You can use these values to reflect your own personal list:

> Determined, kind, achiever, serene, private, works alone, works with others, loyal, affectionate, hygienic, integrity, intellectual, efficient, competitive, responsible, knowledgeable, leader, friendly, honest, independent, cash minded, ethical, democratic, ecological, creative, decisive, community minded, helpful, intimate, orderly, considerate, adventurous.

Choose twelve values that best describe you and write them down. Next, cross seven values out so you're left with five. Was it hard to let go of those seven values? You will sense how important values are when you must eliminate them. You're left with five values. Cross out two more so you're left with three. These three values are highly significant in your life and a part of your true character.

What other values do you believe are part of your character? Add other values, then try eliminating them. You will soon see how important your character is when you reflect on this exercise.

Inventory 3: ABC of recovery from narcissistic abuse

ABC of healing	
A	alpha waves
B	benevolence
C	cry
D	donate blood
E	endorphins
F	flotation tank
G	Gregorian chants
H	hypothalamus
I	immune system
J	Judaism
K	kindness
L	love
M	meditate
N	nervous system
O	oxytocin

P	phosphatidylserine
Q	qi
R	Ralph nuclei
S	serotonin
T	tryptophan
U	ubiquinol
V	vibration
W	wellness
X	xenial behavior
Y	year list
Z	7.8 Hz

Inventory 4: Plan a month of healing tasks

Complete at least one activity each day:

- Pay attention to active breathing
- Have a spinal adjustment
- Cry to release corticotrophin
- Ingest magnesium
- Eat foods containing tryptophan
- Have a hot bath or shower before bedtime
- Listen to relaxing music
- Take fish oil
- Cut back coffee by one cup per day during recovery
- Consider taking a phosphatidylserine supplement
- Ingest vitamin C
- Avoid too much sugar during recovery

- Consider taking ubiquinol
- Consider taking vinpocetine
- Try flotation tank therapy
- Have a food sensitivity test
- Eat chili foods
- Take a twenty-minute walk
- Join an exercise group
- Display xenial behavior
- Sing
- Eat dark chocolate
- Try acupuncture
- Meditate
- Have a massage
- Focus on your love on a pet
- Pray
- Listen to Om, Baroque music or Gregorian chants
- Tap your thymus gland
- Beat a rhythm on a drum
- Complete left brain logical activities
- Listen to binaural beats
- Surround yourself with calm people and synchronize with their thought patterns

Take time to remember who you are. Use the four inventories to reaffirm yourself:

- Inventory 1: Year list
- Inventory 2: Values list
- Inventory 3: ABC list
- Inventory 4: Plan a month of healing tasks

CHAPTER 10

GROWTH

Growth from trauma is a process of finding personal development and positive change amid experiencing loss and sorrow. While trauma can be a challenging and painful experience, it can also provide opportunities for personal growth and transformation. Trauma often prompts individuals to reflect on their lives, values, and priorities. It can lead to a deeper understanding of yourself and what truly matters, helping to clarify your personal goals and aspirations. Going through trauma can cultivate resilience and inner strength. It requires you to navigate difficult emotions, adapt to new circumstances, and find ways in which to cope with profound changes. This resilience can be applied to other areas of life, enabling you to face future challenges with greater strength and resilience.

Trauma can provide you with a new perspective, helping you to appreciate the present moment and the people still in your life. It can foster a sense of gratitude for what remains, leading to a greater appreciation for life's blessings. Experiencing trauma can increase your empathy and compassion towards those who are also going through challenging times. It can deepen understanding of human experience and inspire you to offer support and kindness to others who are grieving. Trauma can be a catalyst for personal growth and transformation, leading you to reassess your values, relationships, and life choices, and prompting you to make positive changes and pursue personal growth opportunities.

You knew who you were before you encountered narcissistic abuse. You may feel like your life will never be the same, but you're still the same person, although with new wisdom and maturity crafted into your character.

During a time of trauma, we can learn to live and trust again.

Elisabeth Kübler-Ross, the world-renowned psychiatrist who lectured on death and dying, made a poignant statement when she wrote, "Beautiful people do not just happen."

Stay strong. Be calm. Use the resources around you to assist in your healing. It's my sincere hope that I have helped make your day a little easier to get through, a little brighter to shine in.

You're not alone and must never feel you're alone. When your recovery from narcissistic abuse makes you feel weary, remember that it's part of a cycle. You can feel differently one minute from now or one hour from now. Tomorrow will be a new day to reach out with hope. Remember to acknowledge your pain and use these strategies to mitigate that pain. Refer to them regularly as you ponder your role in our vast and complex existence.

With love and compassion, I wish you the absolute best in your recovery.

Growth

Had I not known you and seen such beauty
I would never have known the power of love
Nor would I have known the pain of loss
I am who I am today because of you
Our yesterday is my memory today
Through my pain I found growth

Michelle Gregory

SOURCES

1. Aparecido-Kanzler, S., Cidral-Filho, F. J., & Prediger, R. D. (2021, November 24). Effects of binaural beats and isochronic tones on brain wave modulation: Literature review. https://scite.ai/reports/10.24875/rmn.20000100

2. Retrieved August 7, 2023 from Sheenie Ambardar, MD Adult Psychiatrist https://emedicine.medscape.com/article/1519417-overview?form=fpf

3. Retrieved August 7, 2023 from Moss, J, Stephana et al. (2023, April 3). Interventions to improve well-being among children and youth aged 6–17 years during the COVID-19 pandemic: a systematic review. https:// scite.ai/reports/10.1186/s12916-023-02828-4

4. Perry, B., Dr (n.d.). Stress, Trauma and Post-traumatic Stress Disorders in Children. Complex Trauma. https://www.complextrauma.ca/wp-content/uploads/C9-PTSD-in-Children-An-Introduction-.pdf

5. https://associationofanaesthetists-publications.onlinelibrary.wiley.com/doi/10.1111/j.1365-2044.2005.04287.x

6. Rowers' high: behavioural synchrony is correlated with elevated pain thresholds: Emma E. A. Cohen, Robin Ejsmond-Frey, Nicola Knight and R. I. M. Dunbar. Biol. Lett. 2010 6, 106-108 first published online 15 September 2009 doi: 10.1098/rsbl.2009.0670

7. Allan Luks & Peggy Payne: The Healing Power of Doing Good – The Health and Spiritual Benefits of Helping Others. New York: iUniverse.com, 2001

8. *HG Keonig, et al. Am J Psychiatry 155:4, April 1998

9. Rosenzweig, M. R., Bennett, E. L., & Diamond, M. C. (1972). Brain changes in response to experience. Scientific American, 226 (2), 22-29.

10. Health effects of noise on children and perception of the risk of noise: Marie Louise Bistrup, editor. Authors: Marie Louise Bistrup, Staffan Hygge, Lis Keiding, Willy Passchier-Vermeer© 2001 National Institute of Public Health, Denmark

11. John E. Oliver (2005). Encyclopaedia of World Climatology. National Oceanic and Atmospheric Administration. ISBN 978-1-4020-3264-6. http://books.google.com/?id=-mwbAsxpRroC&pg=PA452&lpg=PA452&dq=1.4+billion+lightning+year. Retrieved February 8, 2009.

12. Rubin Naiman, 2006. "Healing Night: The Science and Spirit of Sleeping, Dreaming, and Awakening." Syren Book Company.

13. "Annual Lightning Flash Rate". National Oceanic and Atmospheric Administration. http://sos.noaa.gov/datasets/Atmosphere/lightning.html. Retrieved February 8, 2009.

14. (n.d.). New discovery: How chronic pain changes your brain and personality. Neura. https://neura.edu.au/news-media/media-releases/new-discovery-how-chronic-pain-changes-your-brain-and-personality

15. Fine, T.H., & Turner, J.W., Jr. (1983). The Use of Restricted Environmental Stimulation Therapy (REST) in the Treatment of Essential Hypertension, First International Conference on REST and Self-Regulation, 136-143.

16. Bruce McEwen, Sonia Lupien. Stress: Hormonal and Neural Aspects. Encyclopaedia of the Human Brain, 2003, Pages 463-474 Bruce McEwen, Sonia Lupien

17. Sapolsky RM, Plotsky PM: Hypercortisolism and its possible neural bases. Biol Psychiatry 27:937-952, 1990

18. Sapolsky RM, Uno H, Rebert CS, et al.: Hippocampal damage associated with prolonged glucocorticoid exposure in primates. J Neurosci 10:2897-2902,1990

19. Starks MA, Starks SL, Kingsley M, Purpura M, Jager R: The Effects of Phosphatidylserine on Endocrine Response to Moderate Intensity Exercise. Journal of the International Society of

Sports Nutrition. 2008; 5:11.

20. The Qualitative Report Volume 15 Number 5 September 2010 1243-1269

21. (n.d.). 20. Http://www.Nova.Edu/ssss/QR/QR15-5/kjellgren. Pdf. Neura. https://neura.edu.au/news-media/media-re-leases/new-discovery-how-chronic-pain-changes-your-brain-and-personality

22. Psychotherapeutic Treatment in Combination with Relaxation in a Flotation Tank: Effects on "Burn-Out Syndrome." Anette Kjellgren, Hanne Buhrkall, and Torsten Norlander. Karlstad University, Karlstad, Sweden.

23. Yadav GS, Cidral-Filho FJ, Iyer RB. Using Heartfulness Meditation and Brainwave Entrainment to Improve Teenage Mental Wellbeing. Front Psychol. 2021 Oct 15;12:742892. doi: 10.3389/fpsyg.2021.742892. PMID: 34721219; PMCID: PMC8554296.

24. Binaural beat technology in humans: a pilot study to assess psychologic and physiologic effects. Wahbeh H, Calabrese C, Zwickey H. J Altern Complement Med. 2007 Jan-Feb;13(1):25-32.

25. Elisabeth Kübler -Ross, (1975), Death: The Final Stage of Growth. Simon & Schuster.

Made in United States
Troutdale, OR
09/08/2023

12754686R00030